IT'S TIME TO EAT CHEWY CHOCOLATE COOKIES

It's Time to Eat CHEWY CHOCOLATE COOKIES

Walter the Educator

Silent King Books
A WhichHead Entertainment Imprint

Copyright © 2025 by Walter the Educator

All rights reserved. No part of this book may be reproduced in any manner whatsoever without written per- mission except in the case of brief quotations embodied in critical articles and reviews.

First Printing, 2024

Disclaimer

This book is a literary work; the story is not about specific persons, locations, situations, and/or circumstances unless mentioned in a historical context. Any resemblance to real persons, locations, situations, and/or circumstances is coincidental. This book is for entertainment and informational purposes only. The author and publisher offer this information without warranties expressed or implied. No matter the grounds, neither the author nor the publisher will be accountable for any losses, injuries, or other damages caused by the reader's use of this book. The use of this book acknowledges an understanding and acceptance of this disclaimer.

It's Time to Eat CHEWY CHOCOLATE COOKIES is a collectible early learning book by Walter the Educator suitable for all ages belonging to Walter the Educator's Time to Eat Book Series. Collect more books at WaltertheEducator.com

USE THE EXTRA SPACE TO TAKE NOTES AND DOCUMENT YOUR MEMORIES

CHEWY CHOCOLATE COOKIES

It's cookie time, hooray, hooray!

It's Time to Eat Chewy Chocolate Cookies

Chewy chocolate on the way!

Round and soft and oh so sweet,

A yummy, melty chocolate treat!

Mix the batter, thick and brown,

Stir it up and swirl it 'round.

Add some chocolate, chunks or chips,

Give the spoon a little dip!

Scoop them up and make them round,

Place them gently on the ground,

Oops! I mean the baking sheet!

Soon they'll smell so warm and sweet!

Into the oven, now we wait,

Tick-tock, tick-tock, it's hard to wait!

The smell of chocolate fills the air,

A tasty treat beyond compare!

Ding! The timer says they're done!

Golden brown and baked with fun!

Let them cool, but not too long,

The chocolate smell is much too strong!

Take a cookie, just one bite,

It's Time to Eat
Chewy Chocolate Cookies

Warm and gooey, pure delight!

Chewy, soft, and oh so yummy,

Melts like magic in my tummy!

Dip in milk and take a sip,

Chocolatey goodness on my lip!

Crunchy edges, soft inside,

Best cookie ever, I can't hide!

One for me and one for you,

Maybe three… or maybe two!

Chewy chocolate, let's all share,

Cookies show how much we care!

Let's bake more, it's just so fun!

We can't stop at only one!

Mix and stir, then bake them right,

Chewy cookies, what a sight!

It's Time to Eat Chewy Chocolate Cookies

Cookie time is pure delight,

Morning, noon, or late at night!

Every bite is joy to see,

It's Time to Eat
Chewy Chocolate Cookies

Chewy chocolate, yum for me!

ABOUT THE CREATOR

Walter the Educator is one of the pseudonyms for Walter Anderson. Formally educated in Chemistry, Business, and Education, he is an educator, an author, a diverse entrepreneur, and he is the son of a disabled war veteran. "Walter the Educator" shares his time between educating and creating. He holds interests and owns several creative projects that entertain, enlighten, enhance, and educate, hoping to inspire and motivate you. Follow, find new works, and stay up to date with Walter the Educator™

at WaltertheEducator.com

www.ingramcontent.com/pod-product-compliance
Lightning Source LLC
LaVergne TN
LVHW010622070526
838199LV00063BA/5244